IMAGES
of America

JACKSON COUNTY

IMAGES
of America

JACKSON COUNTY

Michael A. Poe

ARCADIA
PUBLISHING

Published by Arcadia Publishing
Charleston, South Carolina

Library of Congress Catalog Card Number: 2007938753

For all general information contact Arcadia Publishing at:
Telephone 843-853-2070
Fax 843-853-0044
E-mail sales@arcadiapublishing.com
For customer service and orders:
Toll-Free 1-888-313-2665

Visit us on the Internet at www.arcadiapublishing.com

CONTENTS

ACKNOWLEDGMENTS

This book involved over three years of research by the author along with the help of many individuals. I would like to thank all those people who so faithfully helped me in this quest to do a comprehensive history of Jackson County, starting with my mother, Linda Poe, and my proofreader and sister, Kathy Poe.

I would also like to thank the employees at the Jackson County Public Libraries in both Ravenswood and Ripley for their patience and help in collecting pictures and research material, especially Connie Pauley, Lynn Pauley, Maxine Landfried, and the late Ed Rauh. I appreciate their help and encouragement.

I need to thank all the people who contributed pictures and information, starting with the Jackson County Public Library, Fred Rhodes, Sue Smith, David Board, Anne King, David Hyre, Tressie Skeen, Marie Reed, Frank Murray, Bill Mullins, Daniel Bonar, Guy Landfried, Maxine Landfried, John King, Clement Matheny, the Ravenswood Lands Museum, Emily Lamb, Brooks Utt, and the Statts Mill Store.

Finally, I need to thank Ron Reynolds for his guidance and enthusiasm in local history, paving the way for my research, writing, and love of history.

Unless otherwise noted, all images are courtesy of the author.

INTRODUCTION

The mighty Ohio River was the lifeblood of the early settlers and, for many years, it was the only way to reach the western edge of Virginia. The first explorer to enter this untamed region was Robert de La Salle in 1669, the first European to traverse the Ohio River. James Le Tort established the first trading post in 1740 at Letart Falls, near the Jackson/Mason County lines. The Ohio River Trading Company hired Christopher Gist to make an expedition across land into present-day Jackson County in 1752. It was not until 1768 that William John and Lewis Rogers received a land grant for 400 acres, establishing the ownership of property in western Virginia. Then, in 1772, after George Washington's trip through the Ohio Valley, he claimed property along the Ohio River. In 1796, the first families settled at the mouth of Mill Creek near present-day Millwood.

Communities flourished along the Ohio River in the early 1800s due to trade and commerce from keelboats and stern-wheelers. Residents along the river established industries that would benefit them and the ships that stopped at each town. Murraysville became home to one of the largest boatbuilding operations on the western edge, completing more than 150 ships between 1830 and 1890. Sawmills in Ravenswood and Murraysville supplied wood for furnaces and food supplies for crews.

Mill Creek, flowing west to the Ohio, was also utilized by early tradesmen. In 1897, a stern-wheeler carried supplies and passengers from Ripley to Chases Mill. During a flood in 1898, the stern-wheeler made round-trips from Hood's Mill in West Ripley to Millwood to haul supplies. The ship was fueled with wood and coal and took two days to traverse the 26 miles. Eventually the ship ran aground below the Cottageville dam, where its remains are entombed today.

Jackson County has been blessed in growth and prosperity because of the ease of transport. The Ohio River served as an early access to this area, leading to the numerous immigrants settling along its banks. Due to the fact that Jackson County has Parkersburg to the north and Charleston to the south, the trade routes passed through this area. This led areas along the Charleston/Parkersburg Turnpike to excel and grow as more trade moved through the center of the county, allowing towns like Kenna, Sandyville, Lockhart, New Era, and Ripley to cater to the newfound travelers. Boardinghouses and hotels were built in Kenna, Ripley, and Sandyville, and merchants groomed their trade specifically for the era. Early hotels in Ripley had stables for horses and blacksmith shops normally close by, which made shoe repair easy on the traveler.

By 1885, the Ohio River Railroad entered Jackson County, leading to trade extending the entire length of the Ohio River on the western edge of the state. The railroad established depots in Murraysville, Ravenswood, and Millwood along the river. And in 1888, when the route was extended to Ripley, the Ripley and Millcreek Valley Line established depots at Cottageville, Angerona, Evans, and Ripley. The commerce that emerged out of the new form of transportation led to a ground swell of business in the county seat of Ripley. Business owners in Ripley relied on the railroad to deliver all the goods needed to keep their thriving businesses open. Cattle and timber were two of the exports that helped farmers in the center of the county scratch out a living. In 1922, livestock loaded from Ripley totaled four railcars shipped by Parsons and Lee. In the same shipment there were 271,332 pounds of walnuts and 1,872 pounds of hickory nuts, which were shipped to out-of-the-county markets. By 1892, the Ravenswood, Spencer, and Glenville Railroad (RS&G) extended through Crow Summit, Sandyville, Duncan, and Liverpool into Roane County.

By 1909, the natural gas and oil boom had a strong hold in the western edge of the state. United Fuel and Carter Oil Company had a lock on Jackson County; all the first gas pipelines were laid by employees of United Fuel. Farmers welcomed drilling on their lands hoping to cash in on the dollars made from natural gas. Numerous businessmen in Jackson County became extremely wealthy during the natural gas boom in the mid-1920s. The discovery of natural gas and the extending of gas lines throughout the county helped families with heating and cooking, making life easier as the county grew.

Over time, Jackson County became known for the largest small-town Fourth of July celebration in the country. The first Ripley fair was in September 1877, and was also known as the Fall Festival. Early Ripley fairs were held on the fairgrounds, which cover First, Second, and Third Avenues today. There were also fairs held in Evans, Ravenswood, and Kenna, all giving way to the Jackson County Junior Fair held now at the fairgrounds at Cottageville. The Fourth of July celebration held in Ripley grew from a parade covering only Main Street near the courthouse square and widespread entertainment, including local men in boxing matches, wrestling companies, and national performers. Now the celebration includes the arts and crafts fair held at Cedar Lakes and a carnival in Ripley. For year-round entertainment, Jackson County supported opera houses in Ripley and Cottageville. In the 1950s, Sandyville had the Dixie Drive-In Theater, and Millwood had the Raven Drive-In. Automobile racetracks were built at Sandyville near the intersection of Route 21 and Route 56 and at the Evans Fairground.

Jackson County is a melting pot of people, those looking for fertile farmland and others looking for commerce. This is a story of a county that takes diversity in its people and shows how the generations evolved. As each generation is lost so is the history, unless it is documented. The images in this publication show the evolution of Jackson County and the people who were instrumental in today's history. My objective was to show the county from a layman's point of view; these are the people from the hollows and farms that are the backbone of any area. This book is not a complete history of Jackson County, but I hope this volume is enjoyable and informative.

One

CITY AND COUNTRY

In June 1831, the Virginia General Assembly appointed three men—William Spurlock, John Miller, and John McWhorter—to plan the county seat of Jackson County. They met at the home of Joel Sayre on the first Monday of the following September and chose Ripley as the county seat. The courthouse now stands on land donated by Jacob Starcher, and the first courthouse was contracted to be built by James Smith at a cost of $3,700.

Grant District in northern Jackson County was first settled in 1807, when John Dewitt built a cabin at Muses Bottom. The first school at Muses Bottom was erected in 1818, but the first free school was not established until 1865.

In 1837, Elijah Murray and William Hicks purchased 120 acres north of the George Muse tract. By 1838, a boatyard was established and, by 1840, Murraysville was booming.

In southern Jackson County, the community of Kenna was established by G. P. Morrison in the 1880s. At the time, John E. Kenna was a U.S. senator and a friend of the Morrisons. It was due to Kenna's influence that a post office was started, and out of respect for the senator, the community was named Kenna.

In Washington District, the small area of Frozen Camp received its name around 1818. When in midwinter four men came for a hunting trip, they camped and built a fire, but a severe snowstorm and the bitter cold chilled the men through the night. The next morning the men had severe frostbite to their fingers and toes. Helpless and hungry, they traveled several miles to a cabin where they were warmed and fed. From that night on the area was known as Frozen Camp.

In 1833, the first Jackson County Courthouse was built. The jail was 34 feet by 17 feet, and the courthouse was 36 feet by 36 feet. In 1856, the second building was erected by a partnership of Nicholas Bonnett and Joshua Staats at a cost of $7,993. Bonnett and Staats were unable to complete the contract due to an increase in the cost of material and labor. This caused the surety bond Bonnett had posted to be forfeited. Staats died of tuberculosis soon after, and due to the heavy financial losses suffered by the partners, the Staats estate was used in settling up the unpaid accounts. Nicholas Parsons of Mount Alto was commissioned to finish the building. The first floor was used as a jail, and the second story was the courtroom. In 1879, J. T. Blades installed a fireproof records room costing $3,800. This picture is of the second courthouse on the square, c. 1890.

Sandyville is located along Sand Creek in the Ravenswood District. The town supported a mill, a post office, several stores, a church, a school, a hotel, a hospital, a funeral home, a town band, and a regular stop for the RS&G Railroad. This view of Sandyville was taken from Liverpool Road looking west, c. 1890.

Ripley, like other towns in the early 20th century, relied on horses and sleds to navigate the winters. This scene in January 1904 shows Main Street looking east. The large building on the left was Carson's Store, a dealer of Columbus wagons. Further down the street was Morehead and Thomas, a store advertising "Up to date school books."

Leroy is situated in Sandy Valley, along the closed RS&G Railroad. The post office opened on September 21, 1857, with Elijah Baker as postmaster. The Leroy Grade School opened in 1898 with Martha Sayre teaching and remained open until 1947. This 1913 photograph shows the RS&G line heading east, the lumberyard, and the Leroy School.

The Ripley and Mill Creek Valley Railroad had a total of five stops. The first was at Cottageville. The Cottageville depot was two older box cars, one used as a ticket office and the other for freight. The small building on the right was for storing the handcar. (Courtesy of John King.)

B373B4   Main St., Looking East, Ripley, W. Va.

In 1920, Ripley mayor T. Clayton Parsons instituted a system of waterworks and sewage. Mayor Parsons also paved the main streets and was instrumental in building Ripley High School. As seen in this postcard, the streets were dirt, and mud was the overwhelming problem. The first house on the right is at the corner of Main and Maple Streets.

Court Street, Ripley, W. Va.

During the Civil War, the law office of Ulysses Flesher was across from the courthouse. In 1861, while the town was under Union control, Flesher allowed Col. James Guthrie of the 1st Kentucky Infantry to administer the oath of allegiance of the United States to the Southern sympathizers at his law office.

13

In 1809, a New Yorker named Laban Hill attempted to carve out a castle in a rock cliff that overlooked a creek near Donnelly Hill. In 1869, the first postmaster, Hugh Donnelly, named the village Rock Castle. The name was changed to Rockcastle in 1894. This early 1900s photograph shows the church meeting tent and the downtown business area.

In 1852, Thomas W. Simmons moved to Jackson County. By 1868, Dr. Simmons had graduated from the Ohio Valley College of Medicine and, in 1870, he married Sarah Maddox. They resided in Kenna, building this three-story home with the office on the right. By 1915, the third story was removed. The elegant home stood until the 1970s. (Courtesy of Guy E. Landfried.)

The covered bridge in Sandyville was built across Sand Creek around 1875 by Moses Huff. The covered bridge was torn down in 1945 and replaced with a concrete bridge. The foundation stone of this covered structure is still visible today on the north side of the current bridge.

In 1891, a state charter was issued for the Bank of Ripley, which was located at the corner of Main and Church Streets. In 1899, the bank moved into a three-story building on Court Street. The Valley Bank was issued a charter in 1893. By 1907, the banks were competing for business on Court Street. This photograph dates between 1907 and 1915. (Courtesy of Don Flesher collection.)

Cottageville was originally called Wrights Mill, and then changed to Moore's Mill in the mid-1800s. In 1858, founder Daniel Rhodes laid out the streets for Rhodes Mill. After the Civil War, Daniel Rhodes changed the name to Cottage Mills, which was later changed to Cottageville. This photograph is of Main Street in 1925. (Courtesy of Fred Rhodes.)

This aerial view of Ravenswood shows how the city streets were laid out by Henry and Henrietta Fitzhugh in 1837. By 1955, Ravenswood had an airport at the northern edge of town; the landing strip today is now Kaiser Avenue. After the building of Kaiser Aluminum, the town grew to the point that all the land where the airport was located is now homes. (Courtesy of Betty Fowler.)

Angerona was a prosperous town in the mid-1800s. In 1877, while drilling for salt on the Woodruff farm, silver was found. A Pittsburgh company was formed for the sole purpose of testing for silver. Another shaft of 400 feet was sunk, but it was found to be a dry hole. In Angerona, the general store pictured above was the heart of the community. The first storekeeper, William King, later sold out to A. W. and Dave Sayre. In 1909, Jess Sayre bought the store and kept it until 1914. A. W. and Dave Sayre repurchased the store and ran it until it burned in the 1930s. The horse and buggy in this photograph belonged to Harve Sayre. Pictured from left to right are Russ Baker, Harve Sayre, Charley Mullinex, and Alton Brooks. (Courtesy of Don Flesher collection.)

Wilding was originally known as Churchville, and later renamed after minister George Wilding. The Wilding schoolhouse in the center of the photograph was built in 1890. The school also became a summer school for teachers to receive certification. The school closed in the mid-1950s, and the Wilding Post Office closed in 1927.

One of the first car dealerships in Ripley was located on the corner of North and Church Streets in 1935. Bryan Mays opened the Mays Motor Company, which sold Chrysler automobiles. By 1936, the Rhodes Garage occupied the lot and sold Chevrolet automobiles. This 1941 winter photograph shows the banner for the dealership on the left.

The town of Ripley was named in honor of Harry Ripley, a minister who drowned in Big Mill Creek near Chases Mill in 1830. The original owners of the land at Ripley were William John and Lewis Rodgers. They held 400 acres by "corn rights" in 1768. The land was sold to Jacob Starcher in 1816. Starcher laid out the town and donated two acres for the courthouse square. Even though the town was laid out in 1833, it was not incorporated until 1852. Clermont E. Thaw was the first mayor of what was then Ripley, Virginia. In 1868, an amendment was added to the county ballot to move the county seat to Ravenswood, but the attempt failed. This 1920s view exhibits Ripley's growth, including the railroad in West Ripley, Valley Mills, and, in the center, the courthouse.

In 1958, a new streetlight system was installed in Ripley by the R. H. Bouligny Company for the Appalachian Electric Power Company. The new lights were installed on aluminum poles, and the system allowed for the adding of new lights. Mayor Gay Duke turned on the switch of the new lights on March 27, 1959. This photograph shows the first night the new lights were in operation.

The Statts Mill Bridge opened for travel in November 1887. Quincy and Grim contractors did the stonework at a cost $710.40. H. T. Hartley did the woodwork at a cost of $903.95. Enoch Staats was paid $110 for dirt filling. The bridge was moved to Cedar Lakes in 1983. This postcard shows Willa McGinley painting a picture of the structure in the late 1950s.

Two

READING, WRITING, AND ARITHMETIC

In 1796, the General Assembly of Virginia established a law that provided "the schools of each township be managed by three able and honest men." The early schools were free for the first three years then tuition was charged. By 1846, the citizens of the districts had the right to vote on tax increases to support the schools. When West Virginia became a state in 1863, the legislature provided an efficient system of free schools. There were a number of private or subscription schools in Jackson County in the late 1800s. The construction of the school buildings and the employment of a teacher were paid for by the citizens of the area. The teachers were often boarded with families, and the men of the district provided all the labor on the building.

The school term after the Civil War was only two months, and, by 1890, the term was lengthened to four months. The superintendents in the county were responsible for certifying teachers. The early teachers were men because it was believed that a man could maintain discipline. In 1833, the first school commissioners in Jackson County were William Shepherd, Jesse Carney, George Stone, Henry Shearman, Thomas Cain, Jonathon Casto, Gilbert Boswell, Thomas Boggs, John Warth, and Ephriam Evans.

By 1887, the older elementary schools in Ravenswood were overcrowded. H. O. Blennes of Athens, Ohio, was contracted to build a new school with E. W. Wells as the architect. The contract was for the sum of $13,700, and the loans were secured by Robert Brown, J. H. Wetzel, and S. W. Houston. The cost of the final project was $20,000, which included the property. (Courtesy of Don Flesher collection.)

After the 1887 building was constructed in Ravenswood, students had a permanent school to attend. These students were taught by C. E. Keys, Ed Flynn, Margaret Tomlin, Lou Warth, and Maggie Leppert. In 1890, a two-year high school course was offered, with the first class graduating on April 17, 1891. (Courtesy of Don Flesher collection.)

Members of the Round Knob School in 1890 were, from left to right, as follows: (seated) Ida Woodard, Emily Parsons, Hattie Sayre, Georgia Stewart, Gertrude Norris, Nannie Stewart, Verna Morris, Sally Stewart, James Sayre, Elisha Stewart, Everett Parsons, John Stewart, and Jim Parsons; (standing) Trot Parsons, Dick Kay, Orville Sayre, Wesley Stewart, Claude Sayre, Myer Stewart, Frank Searles, Oscar Woodard, Mary Burgess, teacher Hiram Parsons, Kina Stewart, Walter Stewart, Jennings Kay, Gail Sayre, Vaught Sayre, Artie Woodard, Tom Stewart, and Holly Kay. (Courtesy of David Board.)

The Ripley Normal School was owned and operated by A. S. Lee and his cousin C. W. Lee. In order to get a certificate to teach school, a person had to pass the State Uniform Examination. The teacher had to successfully pass an examination on 11 subjects of general interest. (Courtesy of Don Flesher collection.)

The Riverview School was north of Ravenswood near Skull Run. This picture was taken in the spring of 1889. From left to right are (seated) Dollie McKinley, Josie Jackson, Mamie Tumlin, Lucy Bigley, Myrtle Jackson, Alma Jackson, Bessie Gainer, Lona McKinley, Adaline Staats, Dessie Cooper, Thomas Staats, Oscar Cooper, and Luther Jackson; (standing) Isora Gainer, Etta Jackson, Zona Jackson, Ella Staats, Mona Tumlin, Dave Staats, Evalena Bigley, Ben Wheaton, Mary Gainer, Myrtle Staats, James Staats, Herbie McKinley, Robert Staats, Archer Staats, Everett Staats, Robert Wheaton, Tommy Braham, and Jim Staats; (standing in the doorway) Lettie Wheeler and teacher Emmett Tumlin. (Courtesy of Washington Lands Museum.)

The Antioch School was built in 1865 on land owned by Ephraim Sayre. Sayre cut and hewed the logs for the 28-foot-by-30-foot school. In 1882, a new building was erected below the old school. This 1908 picture shows the students and their teacher, John Sayre, in back, along with painter Charley Ramsey. (Courtesy of Don Flesher collection.)

In 1903, the West Virginia State Legislature passed a law establishing a uniform examination for all teachers. Ripley Normal School opened soon after on South Court Street. In 1912, the local newspapers reported that more than 200 students were enrolled under the supervision of A. S. and C. W. Lee. The Normal School remained open until 1926; the building was then used as a graded school.

The Harpold brothers of Statts Mill completed work on the new Gay Elementary School in 1918. The school remained open until a fire destroyed the building in April 1938. The students were able to attend the opening of the new school by September 1938. This photograph from the mid-1940s shows half of Virgil Morris's class enjoying a break.

In 1913, the Ripley Normal School held three terms: the first started in March, the second in April, and the last in June. The students over the summer represented two states and 11 counties. Here the students of the April term take time out for a class picture at the Ripley Fairgrounds. (Courtesy of Jackson County Library.)

Ripley High School had its first football team in 1919. Pictured from left to right are (first row) Clark Kessel, Warren Shinn, Orland Duke, William Staats, Travis Parsons, John Miller, Everette Sayre, and King Parsons; (second row) Creel Casto, Eugene McGrew, Matson King, Dwight Staats, Lovell Parsons, Seaman McGrew, Laco Swisher, Wade Ferguson, and Delbert Staats.

Ripley High School had "Freak Day" for graduating seniors in 1921. Pictured from left to right are the following: (first row) Lucille Swisher, Hazel Hutchison, and Genevieve Starcher; (second row) Jean McGrew, Marion Hood, Hazel Archer, and Hazel Ferguson; (third row) Roberta Keenan, Anna Waybright, Beatrice Hickman, Phylis Landfried, Burton Crow, Velva Faber, Smith Rhodes, Delbert Staats, William Casto, and Julia Progler.

Gilmore High School was built in 1924 by contractor Forrest Hutchinson. The first students attended classes on September 15, 1924, but construction on the school was incomplete. Classes were held from 9:00 a.m. until noon so the carpenters could work the rest of the day. A controversy emerged in 1946 when Gilmore High lost its first-class status as a high school. The school board determined that the cost of a teacher's salary and utilities was too much for the county to pay. Half the students were sent to Ravenswood, and the other half went to Ripley. The legal fight went on until the state superintendent restored Gilmore High's status and reopened it in August 1949. The school remained open until 1965, after which all students either went to Ripley High or Ravenswood High Schools. (Courtesy of Sue Smith.)

Cottageville Grade School was a four-room, two-story building with grades one through eight. The building was used until 1944 when the students were moved into the renovated Union High School. The board of education gave upper classmen their choice of either attending Ripley or Ravenswood High Schools. The Union High School building was demolished in 1985. (Courtesy of Fred Rhodes.)

During Fourth of July celebrations, high school marching bands are the staple of every parade. This photograph shows the Ravenswood Junior High School band resting after a march through Spencer during the parade in 1929. (Courtesy of Washington Lands Museum.)

The Ripley High School football team of 1934 included, from left to right, (first row) Edgar Richards, Clair Wandling, Carroll Rader, Glenn Skeen, John Karr, Ward Winters, Allen Spellman, Lavelle Shinn, William Hall, Ralph Rawley, and Filbert Casto; (second row) Carroll Staats, Parker Shamblin, Leroy Cunningham, Aley Smith, Hickman Williams, Arnold Critchfield, Lowell Pitchford, Edison Parsons, Stanley Pitchford, Edwin Rhodes, Charles Tolley, Milford Casto, Paul Shinn, and James Oldman; (third row) coach Bert Goodwin, Harl Winters, Delbert Casto, Chester Parsons, Talmage Parsons, Charles Kirkpatrick, Carl Blair, Everette Parrish, Marion Parsons, Donald Lowther, Crayton Chancey, Leofrie Wiblin, and Floyd Byer.

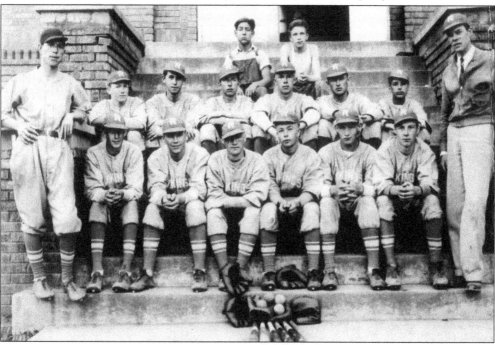

The 1934 Ripley High School baseball team was one of the best at that time. The players, under the direction of coach Bert Goodwin, won the county championship. With wins in their final five games, the team beat Gilmore High with a 30-3 win to take the title.

HIGH SCHOOL AND ANNEX, RIPLEY, W. VA.

Ripley High School began the first term in 1913 with 23 students. Classes were held in one room of the graded school building on Court Street. Briefly, in 1919, classes were held in the Morrison Store building. Credit for building the school goes to Talmage Clayton Parson, B. W. Miller, and Lewis H. Miller. The bond levy in 1920 was approved by only 22 votes in the Ripley District. After the $18,000 bond issue was authorized, work began on building a high school for the Ripley Independent School District. In September 1922, the new Ripley High School opened. The total cost of the project was $31,000. In 1939, construction began on the new vocational agriculture building. By September 1939, the building was complete, and the new classrooms eliminated overcrowding.

Pictured here is 1946–1947 eighth grade class at Ripley Elementary School. From left to right are (first row) teacher Lloyd Stone, Lillian Bias, Jim Rollins, Phyllis Cobb, Wilber Anderson, Mary Lee Barrick, Jim Church, Ida Mae Cunningham, Charles Poling, and principal O. P. Davis; (second row) Betty Fisher, Chester Pullins, Marie Hickman, Max Ludwig, Patty Shontz, and Jim Hunter; (third row) James Bryant, Wilma Casto, Ed Landfried, Earline Guthrie, Sonny Parsons, Viola Southall, Gene Casto, Delores Snyder, Bill Tolley, and Janice Harrison; (fourth row) Jean Harlow, Tom Barnette, Mary Progler, Carl Stone, Grace Kay, Carl Anderson, Jackie Board, Mary Jo Heilman, Mary Stover, and Lena Tippens; (fifth row) Rose Southall, Mary Morgan, Lois Stewart, Naomi Southall, Helen Easter, Sibyl Harper, and Beulah Hicks.

The 1950–1951 Ripley High School basketball team included, from left to right, the following: (first row) Ronald Reynolds, Wilber Anderson, Jim Hunter, Joe Kerwood, Jearl Parsons, Carl Stone, Jack Campbell, and Dickie Casto; (second row) coach Maurice Chapman, Don Anderson, Max Ludwig, Charles Anderson, Bill Hart, Sunny Parsons, and Bill Tolley.

Pictured here is the 1953 Ripley High School football team. From left to right are (first row) Bob Hutton, Roderick Oldham, Max Hart, Bob Anderson, Dickie Landfried, Sattis Parsons, Mutt Anderson, Neil Sayre, Jack Williams, and Gary Skeen; (second row) Bill O'Brien, Gene Waybright, Darrel Wandling, John Jordan, Junior Rowley, Ralph Spellman, David Cummings, Jerry Kyer, Mickey Sayre, and Richard Stutler; (third row) coach Joe Rader, Keith Boggess, Roger Parsons, Fisher Hunt, Ray McNew, Keith Good, Arol Cummings, Dan Casto, Carroll Gandee, Bill Casto, Dick Casto, Jearl Parsons, and coach Dick Mullins. (Courtesy of Don Flesher collection.)

Numerous young ladies have passed through the halls of Ripley High School since the building opened in 1922. These ladies from the early 1950s display the blue and gold spirit. From left to right are (seated) Faye Miller and Sue King; (standing) Dixie Clendenin and Carolyn Harpold. (Courtesy of Don Flesher collection.)

Most young girls dream of either being a cheerleader or a majorette. In 1953, these ladies were majorettes at Ripley High School. From left to right are Jeanne Sallaz, Ada Grace Karr, Jean Shinn, Jo Ann Hardman, Colleen Ellis, Ann Kessel, Shelia Oldham, Helen Hall, and Margaret Staats. (Courtesy of Don Flesher collection.)

Ripley High School had an all-girls singing group that performed at school and social functions. In 1955, the Keynoters were made up of the following students, listed from left to right: Barbara Garnes, Carolyn Harpold, Margaret Staats, Nancy Thomas, Jo Ann Hardman, and Delores Fisher. (Courtesy of Don Flesher collection.)

Pictured here are the Jackson County School bus drivers and board members in 1955. From left to right are the following: (first row) Roscoe Flinn, Conrad McCoy, Frederick Austin, C. Otis Casto, Lavelle Shinn, and driver Webster Parsons; (second row) Carl Paxton, Wade Boswell, Loris Pullins, Everette Hudson, Clovis Parsons, Quino French, Chester Parsons, French Brown, Clayton Rhodes, Clyde Barnette, Bob Morris, Rudolph Parrish, and Phil Hughes; (third row) Ray Wildman, Averill Ray, Clair Hill, Lawrence Morris, Harvey Snyder, Bob Shockey, Aubrey Walters, Dale Lee, Raymond Hughes, Martin Smith, Doyle Burke, and George Smith. (Courtesy of Don Flesher collection.)

Photographer Don Flesher was well known around Jackson County for his zest in capturing the perfect shot. In 1965, he snapped this picture of the Ripley High School majorettes practicing on the football field. From left to right are Carolyn Rader, Linda Bell, Brenda Angus, and Celia Triplett. (Courtesy of Don Flesher collection.)

The class "B" division runner-up for the 1972–1973 year in basketball was Gay Elementary. From left to right are (first row) Michael Poe, Jeff Casto, Harold Whitehouse, Jimmy Wilson, David Whitehouse, Thomas Anderson, and Herbert Hartley; (second row) James Simmons, Jack Simmons, Joseph Reed, Randy Knopp, Chuck Raines, and Everett Casto; (third row) Shirley Frazier, Regina Wilson, Debbie Frazier, Regina Rhodes, Vickie Anderson, and Rhonda Hinzman.

Three

OPEN FOR BUSINESS

The first business interest in Jackson County was as a direct result of the Ohio River traffic. The town of Ravenswood flourished as a result. Sawmills along the river provided wood for the boilers on the stern-wheelers. The town of Murraysville was where men went to seek employment. There were boatyards, a casket factory, and an oar factory. The Ohio River Railroad brought a new kind of business to the area. The stern-wheelers brought passenger traffic and entertainment, but the railroads brought commerce and people. The town of Ripley had sawmills that shipped out railroad ties to replace damaged track and lay new track. All up and down the Ohio Valley, the railroads provided a new means of transport for the farmers and businessmen to distribute products to new markets. By the 1890s, the oil and gas boom was developing in every hill and hollow of Jackson County. This new industry gave landowners a source of income on what was under the ground. Companies like United Fuel and Carter Oil profited, while employing local men to lay pipe and work the wells.

It was not until the late 1950s that Jackson County had a major industry that saw the potential of the Ohio River. When Kaiser Aluminum opened near Millwood, this gave Jackson County a boost in revenue and employment.

William G. Watts opened a general merchandise store on the corner of Virginia and Sand Streets in Ravenswood in March 1880. This picture is of his second store on Sand Street, which he shared with undertaker John Rudman. In 1887, Watts moved to Henrietta and Sand Streets, where he built a large, brick building. During this time, Ravenswood was a shipping point for farmers, trappers, and traders from the surrounding counties. The Watts store was the first store the travelers encountered as they entered Ravenswood. Family members are, from left to right, (first floor) unidentified, William W. Watts, Pearl Watts, Ruby Watts, baby Taylor Watts, unidentified, and John T. Watts; (second floor) Emma Rudman McConnell, three-year-old Fred Rudman, John Rudman, Elizabeth J. Rudman, child Harry Rudman, and Ella McKay. (Courtesy of Washington Lands Museum.)

The Ohio River traffic helped Ravenswood build a strong business climate. Along with the glass works and pottery kilns was the broom factory. In 1880, the owners of the broom factory were brothers Anthony and John Keller. From left to right are the following members of the Keller family: (seated) Ruth, Elizabeth, and Charley; (standing) Anthony, John R., and John. (Courtesy of Washington Lands Museum.)

The Sandyville Mill was modeled after the Cheuvront mills of Harrison County. By 1911, the mill was averaging 500 bushels of wheat and 500 bushels of corn each week. In 1914, the mill was owned by Jack Nutter, John Blosser, and L. D. Rush. Then, in 1936, Sherman Rutan operated the mill and closed it a year later. This photograph was taken in 1886 looking west toward Sandyville.

This photograph shows the Daniel Deming Rhodes store in Cottageville in the 1890s. The Knights of Pythias lodge was upstairs. The man on the right was Abraham McCoy, who was commissioner of revenue in Jackson County from 1856 to 1860. McCoy had his right leg broken during a horse riding accident, and the injury was so serious that the leg had to be amputated below the knee. (Courtesy of Don Flesher collection.)

In 1831, Cyrus McCormick started development of the reaper and mowing machine industry. William Deering became involved in the harvester business around 1870. On May 28, 1898, the Ripley Fairgrounds, which is now First, Second, and Third Avenues, promoted Deering Days. This was when all the new equipment and replacement parts were displayed for farmers and retailers of McCormick-Deering products. (Courtesy of Jackson County Library.)

George and Annie Leonard were merchants in Ravenswood for almost 30 years. As with every family business in the late 1800s, the four Leonard children worked at the store. George passed away in 1907, and Annie passed away in 1908. These ladies were seen leaving the Leonard's store in June 1888. (Courtesy of Betty Fowler.)

One of the prominent stores in Ripley in the early 1900s was the Starcher Brothers on the corner of Court and North Streets. Owners were Samuel G., Charles W., Homer G., and Franklin F. Starcher. The store sold groceries, fine china, and glassware. The store was so large that, at one time, there were a dozen employees.

Pictured here is the C. S. and A. S. McCoy hardware store in Cottageville, *c.* 1900. The McCoy store was a distributor of Syracuse Plows. The company was well known for the slat moldboard plow. The Syracuse Chilled Plow Company, created in 1876, was purchased by the John Deere Company in 1910. (Courtesy of Don Flesher collection.)

Odenna Profitt Oldham was born in Parchment Valley in 1868 and married Lenna McKown in December 1897. In 1901, they had a store beside the Bank of Ripley on Court Street. This photograph, taken when the store was on Main Street, shows O. P. and Lenna and an unidentified girl. (Courtesy of Don Flesher collection.)

This elegant home was on the corner of Church and Sycamore Streets. Daniel Greer built the home in 1899; he was one of Jackson County's more prominent citizens. Greer served four terms on the Ripley City Council and was on the board of education. By 1906, he had opened the D. W. Greer and Company Store and held real estate investments. In 1913, he built a two-story building on Main Street beside the W. T. Greer home. On January 2, 1920, Greer sold the Main Street building to O. J. Morrison and Company. By 1936, Greer sold his home to Bryan and Foster Mays, who opened the Mays Funeral Home. The Mays brothers sold the building to Dr. Richard Camden Starcher in 1939. Starcher moved the building to the corner of North and Sycamore Streets, where he opened the Starcher Hospital. The hospital had 24-hour service and 10 beds. The hospital closed in 1956. This photograph from 1906 shows the original United Brethren Church in the background.

The town of Liverpool had a general store on the border of Jackson and Roane Counties. The building was constructed in the late 1800s during the railroad boom. The store was the center of all activities, as seen in this New Year's Day 1910 photograph. Some of the owners over the years were Bud Smith, Ronald Smith, the Brown family, and Ray Francis. (Courtesy of Brooks Utt.)

Rudolph Starcher is seen stopping at the general store owned by Everett Rhodes at Gay. The store was only 18 feet by 30 feet in size, but it contained everything from candy to a drug department. The Rhodes family members were farmers who only opened the store when someone stopped and needed merchandise. (Courtesy of Tressie Skeen.)

In 1909, United Fuel Gas Company started laying the gas lines for Jackson County. In 1911, gas pipe was hauled to Ripley by the Ripley and Mill Creek Valley Railroad. Teams of oxen roamed the streets hauling the heavy rigs. The new line was laid in the Ripley Improvement Company addition, now known as Charleston Drive. (Courtesy of Washington Lands Museum.)

The veterinarian office in Ravenswood was located at 409 Sand Street. This picture was taken in 1912. From left to right are William J. McMaster, Dr. J. A. McMaster, and Mrs. J. A. McMaster. Before 1912, this building was a meat market owned by Tom Compston, with the Citizens Telephone service upstairs. (Courtesy of Washington Lands Museum.)

On January 28, 1916, work began on the Sandyville Gasoline Dryer Plant owned by United Fuel. The first piece of property was bought in 1915 for $700, and, in 1917, another acre was purchased for $175. In 1919, a right-of-way was purchased for $200. Men came from all over the country seeking work, and many were employed originally as carpenters, sawing timber for the buildings. The RS&G Railroad supplied the equipment for the plant. By 1921, the railroad was hauling in tankers of fuel to be refined at the Sandyville plant. The plant was sold to the Virginian Gasoline and Oil Company, but the plant was repurchased in 1949 by United Fuel. By 1954, the plant was producing propane and butane and had approximately 20 employees. This photograph is of the plant *c.* 1925; railroad tankers can be seen in the distance, and Sandyville is on the left.

The A. M. Carson store was originally located in West Ripley near the railroad depot. In 1894, Carson moved to the corner of Court and Main Streets. This customer credit slip is No. 500, dated June 30, 1913. Along with repaying the timothy seed, this customer was charged 10¢ for interest.

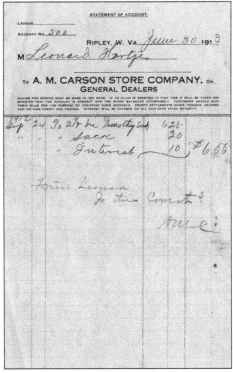

In 1840, Joel Sayre built the Valley Mill on the western bank of Mill Creek. Thirteen years later, Sayre sold the mill to John McGrew, who updated the mill by installing two new sets of stone burrs. During the Civil War, McGrew sold the mill to the D. K. Hood family, who ran the mill until it closed in 1930. (Courtesy of Don Flesher collection.)

Main St. Ripley, W.Va.

In 1855, Edward Maguire opened his new hotel, calling it Washington Hall. The first December dance of 1855 was a gala affair at Washington Hall. The men were enticed by the well-stocked bar and a fine meal. The price for the gala was $1.50 per man, and the women were admitted free. The hotel was located on the Gilmer, Ripley, and Ohio Turnpike, later to be Main and Court Streets. Around 1860, the name was changed to the Maguire Hotel. The hotel also provided a two-horse hack, which was available to carry customers around Ripley. During the Civil War, the Maguire was a dining hall for Union soldiers. On March 25, 1917, George Johnson opened a barbershop in the building beside the Maguire. This photograph was taken on September 8, 1917. The building was razed and later became the First National Bank.

The Farmers Building and Loan Association opened in Ravenswood in 1905 at 212 Walnut Street. It was organized by George W. Park with help from his son Robert. It changed later to Farmers Federal Savings and Loan. John R. Keller sold insurance, but the client picked the insurance company. Pictured here are George W. Park (left) and John R. Keller. (Courtesy of Washington Lands Museum.)

Ravenswood House was built by A. J. Kenney about 1848. During the Civil War, Jenkins's Rebels looted the hotel. Kenney brought suit against Jenkins and collected enough money to cover his losses from the raid. The hotel had 49 rooms and a large veranda. The hotel was on the Ohio River bank overlooking the flowing waters and remained open until the 1960s.

The first post office in Ravenswood was established on July 19, 1839, with Joseph Holden as postmaster. At that time, Ravenswood received all mail from the traffic on the Ohio River. This photograph was taken in 1927 with the post office at that time being on the corner of Washington and Mulberry Streets. (Courtesy of Don Flesher collection.)

In 1847, Nathan Ong laid out the town of Angerona on the south side of Big Mill Creek. Early businesses included two general stores, a post office, sawmill, gristmill, tannery, and a blacksmith shop. The mill was owned by A. W. and Dave Sayre but was run by O. A. Brooks. The man on the porch is O. A. Brooks and the man walking is Samuel Brooks. (Courtesy of Don Flesher collection.)

The Mallory blacksmith shop was at Cottageville near the mill. Along with the rigors of the job of being a blacksmith, the Mallory family also ran the livery stable. This early-1920s photograph shows the entire family taking time from work to pose for the camera. (Courtesy of Don Flesher collection.)

In 1907, the first natural gas field was discovered near Gay by the Carter Oil Company. The gas was found in the salt sand at a depth of 1,760 feet. In 1921, oil discovery at Gay prompted a surge of small oil fields. Oil was discovered in the Cow Run Rock formation at a depth of 1,350 feet. (Courtesy of Tressie Skeen.)

The Ravenswood Grocery Company opened in 1907 as a wholesaler of products for merchants in Jackson and surrounding counties. Salesmen would travel to isolated stores delivering goods at wholesale prices, bringing products these merchants would normally not provide. The building was strategically located beside the railroad tracks and only one block from the Ohio River. This allowed for easy shipments from manufacturers and suppliers. (Courtesy of Don Flesher collection.)

In 1869, David Somerville bought a store in Ravenswood owned by David Mills. Somerville remodeled and added on to the store until he had a 32-room hotel. David Somerville named the hotel Victoria, after his daughter. The hotel catered to all the railroad traffic. The Victoria Hotel closed when the passenger service ended on the Ohio Valley Railroad. (Courtesy of Don Flesher collection.)

This horse-driven hearse was owned by Twiggs Funeral Home in Ravenswood. In 1922, the funeral home was located on the 200 block of Race Street. The early funeral homes either used flat wagons or elaborate hearses like the one in the photograph. (Courtesy of Don Flesher collection.)

The Board Mill opened in 1920 at the fork of Gay Road and Elk Fork Road. The mill sat beside a small stream across from the W. C. "Cleve" Rhodes home. The mill was owned by Okey Board, and along with his family, he operated it until 1925. (Courtesy of David Board.)

One of the first wells in Gay was the Hinzman well, at a depth of 2,628 feet. In 1909, the Elza Anderson well on Billy's Run was drilled by the Carter Oil Company to a depth of 1,792 feet. Here Cyril Rhodes and Oris McCrady are working to dismantle a small derrick on Brush Run. (Courtesy of Marie Reed.)

All sawmill work is dangerous but especially when the work is done by steam engines. In 1924, a sawmill on Hartley Run at the Carder Farm used a gas-powered engine. The employees were Chester Utt, Henry Utt, Ray Utt, and George Kuel. (Courtesy of Brooks Utt.)

The Valley Bank was chartered in 1893, located in a building on the corner of Court and North Streets. The Valley Bank moved into a building on Court Street in 1907. On August 3, 1915, the bank surrendered its charter to the State of West Virginia. The First National Bank of Ripley opened on August 4, 1915. In 1927, the Citizens State Bank merged assets with the First National Bank. After the merger, the new bank erected a building on the corner of Main and Court Streets. In 1966, the First National Bank had outgrown the old building, and the bank bought the property at the corner of Court and North Streets. The lot had been the Starcher Hospital, and is today the United National Bank. Employees in 1927 were, from left to right, George Straley, Margaret Walker, and Howard Kerwood. (Courtesy of Don Flesher collection.)

The St. Dennis Flour Mill was in Ravenswood at the corner of Water and Sycamore Streets. In 1901, the mill was operated by Art Ritchie and Elmer Cross. The mill had track laid to the Ohio River, which was used to truck the grain from barges. In 1920, the mill became the Knotts, Shrimplin, and Wolfe Roller Mill.

The small community of Liverpool had a boardinghouse in 1925 built by the Heck Oil Company. The boardinghouse was called the "Big Hungry" because of the superb eating. The building was only open five years and was torn down in 1930. (Courtesy of Brooks Utt.)

Harpold Brothers store was located in the J. A. McIntosh building on the corner of Washington and Walnut Streets in Ravenswood. Harpold Brothers offered doors, windows, nails, roofing, wagons, gasoline engines, barb wire, rugs, and furniture for every room. Although the store is closed, the building is still in use. (Courtesy of Don Flesher collection.)

The corner of Main and Church Streets is the main intersection in Ripley. The Ripley Hotel was originally built on the corner, and in 1920, Dr. B. F. Rhodes sold the hotel to David Raines for $7,000. The Sandborn maps were drawn for fire insurance companies; each map provided details on structures in cities and towns across the United States. The map of Ripley in 1933 shows the Esso station erected and in business.

On August 12, 1937, the Ripley Livestock Company opened a new livestock market in west Ripley near the railroad depot. The first day saw more than $20,000 worth of livestock sold, with hogs selling for 13¢ per pound and steers at 12¢ per pound. Livestock was trucked in and hauled out in railroad cars to the Parkesburg market. The property was leased in 1951 and became the Jackson County Livestock Market Inc. The officers were W. A. Lee, Estel Simmons, and R. E. Staats. The stock for the new company was owned by farmers and livestock producers. By the end of 1951, a court case was set against the property because the original company forfeited on more than $48,000 in unpaid invoices. The case was not settled until 1956 when a Charleston company took over the running of the market. The first sale was on March 15, 1956, after a five-year court battle.

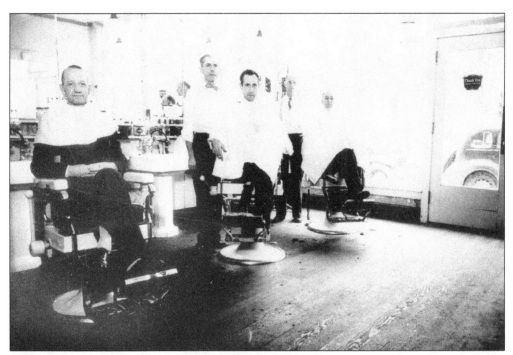

The Casto Barbershop on Main Street in Ripley opened in 1925. This picture shows the barbershop as full on March 2, 1936. The shop is open today with very little change to the interior. From left to right are Grover Castrup, Tack Casto, Wendell Casto, Coop Starcher, and Ed Hawk.

On March 5, 1937, company officials of the Alpine Theater group announced that a movie theater would be built in Ravenswood. The company bought property owned by D. E. Cole on Washington Street. The company was to install the most modern equipment at the time. In April 1951, the Jur Theater Circuit leased the building and held the lease until the theater closed.

Kenna had numerous stores over the years. In the mid-1920s, Foster and Freda Mays opened a general merchandise store. The Mays Store sold almost any product needed at that time. This 1938 photograph shows a porch full of Ball Brand shoes. These were the four- and five-buckle pullover boots. (Courtesy of Maxine Landfried.)

This winter shot on Walnut Street in Ravenswood looking east shows Harpold Brothers hardware and the Farmers Building and Loan Association. The building housing the Farmers Building and Loan Association was built in 1905. It remained until 1973 when the City of Ravenswood bought the building; it is now city hall. (Courtesy of Jackson County Library.)

The post office in Ripley was established on January 31, 1832, with the name Jackson Courthouse. The first postmaster was Robert Lowther. On March 31, 1893, the name changed to Jackson. Then, on September 15, 1897, the name was finally changed to Ripley. The post office in 1922 was on the corner of Court and North Streets. By 1939, the U.S. government had allotted $75,000 for the purchase of property and constructing a new building. The Kessel Hospital building lot on Main Street, owned by the Greer heirs, was finally purchased. The old Kessel Hospital building was moved to the high school property. The new Ripley Post Office was completed by September 1941, and postmistress Winnie Kerwood opened the doors. The building is still in use.

This scene of Washington Street in Ravenswood shows the Slaven Store Company that dealt in shoes, dry goods, floor coverings, and ready-to-wear clothes. The two-story building back off the street was the Ravenswood Cash Store. Beside it, in the small building, was J. B. Shockey's Jewelry Store. (Courtesy of Jackson County Library.)

Okey Board and his son Russell opened a mill on Second Avenue in Ripley in 1933. Along with a blacksmith shop at the rear of the building, this business lasted for 32 years. The machinery used was made by the American Midget Marvel Flour Mill, c. 1945. When the mill closed in 1975, all of the equipment was sold. (Courtesy of David Board.)

On December 5, 1949, Jackson County was awarded the honor of housing the conference center for the Future Farmers and Future Homemakers of America. The 231-acre Easter farm was purchased and cleared, and construction started in 1950. Work on the lakes started in 1951, with the main lodge and cottages being constructed in 1953. By 1954, the bridge was built connecting Cedar Lakes Drive to the conference center, along with the walking bridges that crossed the central lakes. The camp opened in 1955 and was named Cedar Lakes in 1957. In 1959, members of the West Virginia chapter of the Daughters of the American Revolution gathered to formally dedicate the new amphitheater. The outdoor theater cost $2,000 to build and could seat 500 people. The amphitheater was completed in 1962 and could seat 1,200 people. Today there are few signs the outdoor theater ever existed.

The Y Restaurant in Sandyville was operated by Virginia Smith from 1948 to 1958. After Virginia Smith left the restaurant business in 1958, it remained open under new managers until July 4, 1959. Carl E. Smith, Inc. pipeline contractor operated in back of the service station from 1946 to 1970. (Courtesy of Sue Smith.)

The Highway Motel in Ripley opened on April 10, 1952, and was owned by W. E. Oldham. The Oldham children cleaned the rooms and did laundry. In 1955, the Oldhams added eight more units to the motel. On November 22, 1957, the motel was sold to R. D. Sands of Hamlin. Today the property is the Tom Peden Chevrolet dealership.

Jim Williams, Village Rest, Ripley, W. V. 1955

The Candy Corner on the corner of Main and Church Streets has been a restaurant since 1922. In March 1947, Minnie Hunter sold the restaurant to Robert W. Hunter and William R. Hinzman, and the name was changed to the Village Dairy Store. By September 1947, Jim and Audel Williams bought the restaurant and changed the name to the Village Restaurant. Mr. Williams made national news in 1950 when he bought the champion ham of the Little Kanawha Ham and Bacon Show in Parkersburg at a price of $36.60 per pound. The prize ham was served on Easter Sunday with the special guest being the family of the boy who raised the hog. By 1955, Williams had expanded the building and installed air conditioning along with a parking lot behind the building. At one point, in 1955, eighteen waitresses worked to keep up with the growing business. In 1959, the Village Restaurant added a catering service that could serve 300 people. (Courtesy of John King.)

Construction on Jackson General Hospital began in the early 1960s. The hospital was dedicated on November 15, 1964, at a total cost of $1 million. The staff consisted of 47 employees and 5 doctors caring for 41 beds. The first baby born was a boy to Mr. and Mrs. Harold Lupardus.

Kenna got a new service station in 1954, built and operated by Daniel Landfried. The Landfrieds also built the new home on the hill above the station. Daniel operated the station from 1954 to 1958. Today this lot is the Clendenin's Used Cars dealership. (Courtesy of Charles Landfried.)

Four

GETTING FROM
HERE TO THERE

The early settlers used old Native American paths to cross the county in the western edge of Virginia. Work began on the Glenville, Ripley, and Ohio Turnpike in 1848 and was completed in 1853, running from Weston to Ripley. The road was dirt and only 15 feet wide at the widest spot; there were no bridges over the entire road.

The city of Ripley had dirt streets until 1920 when the first paving was contracted to run from the West Ripley Bridge down Main Street to Church Street. The paving cost $1.56 per yard, and the total cost was $3,000. In 1937, the state road commission used gravel to cover the county roads because more miles could be built cheaper and faster.

The automobile in Jackson County was more of a luxury than a necessity. The first automobile accident to occur in Ripley was in 1911 when Dr. Travis Parsons ran his touring car into a ditch near the opera house on North Street. Dr. Travis Parsons and his son-in-law were uninjured but the right front wheel of the car was demolished.

Bartholomew Fleming started a ferry service in Ravenswood in 1832. The ferry ran from Ravenswood to Ohio and back for more than 150 years. The town of Ravenswood was established because of the river traffic and the need for service along the Ohio route.

Today interstate traffic passes through the county without any knowledge of the history and legends that shaped the people of Jackson County.

Construction on the Ripley and Mill Creek Valley Railroad began in 1885. William T. Greer, John Greer, Kenna Hood, and Jim Poling organized the company with William T. Greer as the first president. It was under his management that the railroad was built and the first engine purchased. The tracks covered 13 miles, winding its way along Big Mill Creek to intersect with the Ohio River Railroad near Millwood. The first train entered Ripley in September 1888 during the Ripley Fair; the engine was a Tom Thumb–type. This photograph shows the crowd gathered to see the train, with photographer Susan King preparing to capture the event. The depot was moved back 100 yards and turned parallel to the tracks in 1914, and where the Carson Building stood is now an empty lot. The depot is still in use today with very little changing from its original state. This intersection today is State Route 33 and Klondyke Road.

REGULAR MARIETTA, PARKERSBURG AND RAVENSWOOD DAILY PACKET.

Leaves RAVENSWOOD Daily at 11 P. M.   Leaves PARKERSBURG Daily at 3 P. M.

Murrayville May 1886.

M Thompson 4d Jackson

TONY MELDAHL, Master.
J. H. BROOKHART, Clerk.   To Steamer **Harry D. Knox**, Dr.

Through Receipts given for Freights to all points on the Muskingum and Little Kanawha Rivers.

Marks.	To Freight on	Freight.	Charges.	Amount.
King 4d Syw Murrayville	75 Kegs Powder	4 50		

The boatyard in Murraysville was established in 1838 by Elijah Murray. Over a period of 52 years, approximately 150 steamboats and towboats were built at the Flesher boatyard. As shown in this receipt ticket dated 1886, Murraysville was a regular stop for the Marietta, Parkersburg, and Ravenswood Daily Packet.

In April 1939, the State Road Commission announced that construction would begin on a new river road extending from Parkersburg south to Ravenswood. The highway would start with a court case because the state was going to exercise the right of eminent domain on 12 pieces of property. This picture is of the straight stretch at Muses Bottom where Pete Gould Excavating is located today. (Courtesy of Daniel Bonar.)

The building of Route 2 was a slow and tedious process, with 10 miles of road taking two years to complete. The contract for the 4.702-mile section north of Sherman was contracted to the Keeley Construction Company of Clarksburg at a cost of $207,346. This photograph shows the cliff two-tenths of a mile south of Skull Run. (Courtesy of Daniel Bonar.)

During World War II, construction on Route 2 was halted due to a lack of men and equipment. In June 1949, Boso and Ritchie got the contract to finish a 3.6-mile section from Belleville and Neptune Hill. The award was for $225,901, which included drainage and grading. This photograph was taken on Milhoan Ridge looking north toward the Ohio River. (Courtesy of Daniel Bonar.)

One of the many ships built at Murraysville in 1880 was completed in Wheeling and named the *Sidney*. The stern-wheel packet was 221 feet by 35.5 feet by 5.5 feet. It ran the St. Louis line until 1921 and was then renamed the *Washington*. It operated until 1937 and was dismantled in 1938.

The Ohio River Railroad Company first entered Jackson County in 1884. The project was the idea of Sen. Johnson Camden of Parkersburg. The line was finished, running from Parkersburg to Point Pleasant, in 1886. By 1887, six trains departed Ravenswood daily, with passenger service ending on January 31, 1957. (Courtesy of Don Flesher collection.)

The Ravenswood, Spencer, and Glenville Railroad was incorporated on April 10, 1860. But the line was not completed until January 4, 1892, with the Civil War and problems with local farmers delaying the project. This is one of the RS&G trains, a steam B8, 4-6-0, 10-wheeler that stopped at the Ravenswood depot in 1946. (Courtesy of John King.)

Before the Ohio Valley Railroad track was laid in Ravenswood, negotiations were conducted between the railroad and Judge Robert Brown. The railroad agreed to construct a four-and-a-half-foot fence and make cattle guards and crossings. The Ohio Valley Railroad covers 28.5 miles along the Ohio River. The line was sold on August 1, 1901, to the Baltimore and Ohio Railroad. (Courtesy of Don Flesher collection.)

The RS&G Railroad opened in January 1892. One of the stops after 1916 for the tanker cars was the Sandyville Gasoline Dryer Plant. The plant relied entirely on the railroad to transport the fuel before and after processing. This photograph was taken in 1917.

On January 7, 1966, the West Virginia State Road Commission opened the exchange linking Route 33 in Ripley and I-77, extending an 18.77-mile section through Jackson County. The new interstate system required additional bridges and the expansion of Route 33. This photograph shows the new bridge crossing Mill Creek running east toward Ripley.

Federal Route 21 near Ripley, W. Va.

The old Charleston pack horse trail ran from Mineral Wells to the Kanawha salt springs. This trail ran north to south through Jackson County before Ripley was founded. Later it was named the Parkersburg and Charleston Turnpike, running south of Ripley along the current Cedar Lakes Drive. The early turnpikes had turnstiles or poles every five miles that had to be turned to allow the traveler to pass. Federal Route 21 from Parkersburg to Charleston was completed in July 1935, costing the state of West Virginia $2.8 million in paving and bridge building. Before the State Road Commission was established, each county had to maintain the highways. Parkersburg is 36.47 miles to the north of Ripley, and Charleston is 38.56 miles to the south. Federal Route 21 runs from Mineral Wells in Wood County to Florida. This early picture of Route 21 in 1934 shows how desolate the driving would be through Jackson County.

The Ravenswood, Spencer, and Glenville Railroad was known in its early days as a passenger line. Some of the nicknames given the line by its customers were the old "Rob, Steal, and Gouge" or the "Rub, Snuff, and Grin." This was the last steam engine, a B18, 4-5-0, 10-wheeler, to run the Ravenswood, Spencer, and Glenville line. (Courtesy of John King.)

Bartholomew Fleming operated the first ferry service in Ravenswood on the Ohio River. Fleming navigated the ferry to the head of Big Sand Creek around 1832. With help from his descendents, it remained in operation until the 1920s, after which various owners used the ferry to shuttle people across the Ohio River until 1978. (Courtesy of Jackson County Library.)

Construction on the Ripley and Mill Creek Valley Railroad was delayed three years because the 13-mile stretch had 13 bridges. A "Y" was cut into the Ohio River line so engines could be turned. Once in Ripley, the train would cross onto a second set of tracks that led to the turntable. Here a B8 No. 2028 train, No. 961, enters the station on December 1, 1949. (Courtesy of John King.)

The National Interstate System came out of the Federal Highway Act of 1956. Interstate 77 is the longest interstate in West Virginia, covering 187.21 miles and costing more than $1 billion to complete. The construction in this picture shows the Ripley and Route 33 exchange looking north, c. 1961. (Courtesy of Don Flesher collection.)

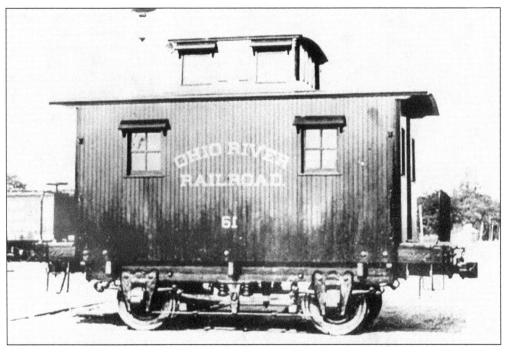

The Ohio River Railroad used four-wheel bobbers until the early 1900s when they changed to eight-wheel cabooses. The first cabooses were wood shacks built on flat cars, used by brakeman to watch the rear of the train. A cupola was later added to the roof to improve vision. The car received the name bobber because it would "bob" down the tracks. (Courtesy of John King.)

When the Ohio River Railroad was opened for traffic on June 16, 1884, the line ran from Wheeling to Parkersburg. Construction on the southern section running to Point Pleasant began in 1885 and ended in 1886. This photograph shows one of the first 4-4-0 trains to stop at Ravenswood in 1886. (Courtesy of John King.)

In January 1916, a Ravenswood, Spencer, and Glenville passenger train wrecked at Crow Summit. It was determined that an old rail, ice, weight, and speed derailed the train. The only injury was to a fireman, but it was not serious. Rev. J. L. Ayers, a passenger in the coach car, said, "The shades of eternity flitted across my mind before the car obeyed the law of inertia and stood still."

On December 1, 1949, a B&O mixed train, No. 81, with five cars and a caboose entered the Ripley depot. This was the longest train to travel the route of the Ripley and Mill Creek Valley line. This photograph was taken at Millwood while the train was preparing for the excursion to Ripley. (Courtesy of John King.)

COMPLIMENTS OF - VILLAGE DAIRY STORE - RIPLEY, W. VA.

OLD COVERED BRIDGE - Constructed 1883 - Now in use over Millcreek
4 Miles South of Ripley, W. Va. - Just off Route U.S. 21

The Chase Mill Bridge was constructed in 1883, four miles south of Ripley near the old Charleston and Ripley Turnpike. Chase's Mill was named for Henry Chase; he served in the 22nd Virginia Infantry during the Civil War. Chase, along with Thomas Windon, built a gristmill on the Chase farm. In 1962, the remains of the old covered bridge fell into Mill Creek.

Pictured here from left to right are engineer D. C. Davis, fireman J. R. Montgomery, supervisor of locomotive operations D. J. Ferrell, conductor J. A. Thompson, and freight agent Charles Flesher. Flesher became the agent in Ripley on August 19, 1896. He retired after 56 years and 9 months of service on May 1, 1953. This photograph is of the first diesel train in Ripley in December 1953. (Courtesy of John King.)

The Gordon C. Greene was built at the Howard Shipyard in Jeffersonville, Indiana, in 1923 for the Eagle Packet Company. By 1925, the steamer was running Mardi Gras trips and continued until 1930 when the Depression forced the company to retire the steamer. In 1936, a second sun deck was added, and passengers along the Ohio River were paying as high as $275 per person for accommodations. The steamer appeared in several famous movies: *Steamboat around the Bend*, *Gone With the Wind*, and *The Kentuckean*. In 1961, the ship was sold for $49,100 and renamed the *River Queen*. It then became a restaurant boat, with a theater, bingo, and amateur acts. The steamer sank in St. Louis on December 3, 1967. The route past Ravenswood was popular for the local residents, allowing for an entertaining view of life on a steamer. (Courtesy of Jackson County Public Library.)

Five

PEOPLE AROUND
THE COUNTY

The first settlers along the Ohio River were the Native American tribes more than 14,000 years before the first European explorer reached the Ohio Valley. The Adena Indians had settled along the fertile bottoms and relied on the excellent hunting. Mounds have been discovered all along the Ohio River, and these discoveries led archaeologists to determine the early people of this region.

There are differing opinions as to who was the first white explorer. The only fact is that James Le Tort established a trading post at Letart Falls in 1740. Then, in 1749, the French explorer Celoron de Blainville traversed the Ohio River, burying lead plates along the river, one being at the mouth of the Kanawha River. The first explorer to travel overland to this edge of the state was Christopher Gist in 1752 while working for the Ohio Trading Company.

By 1810, the settlers that entered Jackson County decided to live along the river. Most lived at Millwood, Cottageville, or Ravenswood with a brave few venturing inland toward Ripley. The river access and traffic made the fertile land near the river the only possible option for settlers at that time.

The social makeup of Jackson County has evolved over the years to welcome the many people who have immigrated to call this area home. From the first settlers whose families still have descendents in the area, to the families who are transplants here, this chapter is devoted to all.

George Washington first explored western Virginia on October 28, 1770. On December 15, 1772, Washington was granted land by King George III of England for serving in the French and Indian War. Washington claimed 2,448 acres in Ravenswood, 4,395 acres at Millwood, and 2,314 acres above Murraysville. After Washington's death, his heirs had the land surveyed and divided. Two of the heirs founded Ravenswood or "Washington's Woods." (Courtesy of Jackson County Public Library.)

In August 1935, the Works Progress Administration announced that a swimming pool would be built in Ripley. The federal agency allotted $6,375.12 for the project, and the pool was to be built at the end of West Street on the old creamery lot. The official opening of the new 45-foot-by-105-foot pool was on August 30, 1936.

The Sandy Post Office was established January 31, 1833, with Warren Reed as the first postmaster. The name was changed on May 23, 1892, to Sandyville. The store and post office stood where the New Era Garage was later built. The current Sandyville Post Office is near the site of the original building.

These young men of Lockhart take advantage of spring days in 1946 to bike ride near the Murray homestead. From left to right are Clellie Maddox, Frank Murray, Bernard Lockhart, Lowe Wagner, Joe Campbell, and Larry Dean Wilson (on the handlebars.) (Courtesy of Frank Murray.)

Pictured here is the Ravenswood City Band in 1900 on the steps of the 1887 school. Shown from left to right are the following members: (first row) George Hoyt Bennett and None Bare; (second row) Bert Earnest, Ed Harpold, Otta Emerick, Frank Harpold, and J. A. Petty; (third row) Walter Emerick, Robert Brown, Frank Fleming, and Earl Shank. (Courtesy of Washington Lands Museum.)

Native American fighter and scout Jesse Hughes first came to Jackson County in 1820 and settled near Sandyville. After losing rights to the property, he moved south of Ravenswood. Hughes died in 1829, and on May 30, 1924, the Daughters of the American Revolution had this monument erected in his honor. (Courtesy of Don Flesher collection.)

This stately home in Ravenswood, called the Cedars, was built in 1840 by Ephraim Wells. Wells's son-in-law, Judge Robert Brown, bought the home in 1876. A son, Charles Brown, inherited the property. Charles, along with his wife, Frances, and daughter, Helen, enjoy a carriage ride in this 1890 photograph. Helen Brown Fowler lived in the home until 1948. (Courtesy of Jackson County Library.)

In 1916, the employees of United Fuel laid gas line along the Jackson County line near Gay. Each worker was given a 16-foot section to work using a pick, shovel, and mattock. Employees sometimes had to walk five or more miles to work each morning. Workers were paid 20¢ per hour, for 10-hour days, six days a week. (Courtesy of Judy O'Conner.)

The last public hanging in the state of West Virginia took place in Ripley on December 16, 1897. John Morgan was the condemned man who was convicted of murdering a widow, Chloe Greene, and her two children, Jimmy Greene and his half-sister, Matilda Pfost. Morgan escaped from the Jackson County jail and made his way toward Roane County. He became lost and, when asking directions of a preacher, was easily recognized and recaptured. Local businessman O. J. Morrison stated he'd give Morgan a new suit for the event if Morgan would tell the story of his crime for Morrison to publish. The hanging lured press from as far away as New York. After the hanging, the state legislature passed a law stating that all executions were to be held at the state prison at Moundsville. The press at that time stated that the hanging was a carnival atmosphere with families picnicking on the grounds. (Courtesy of David Board.)

The community of Gay had several stores with one belonging to James McCrady. His store opened in 1912 beside the McCrady home. James McCrady also owned stores in Staats Mill in Jackson County and Clarence in Roane County. The McCrady store closed in 1926 when James passed away. This photograph shows James on the left and his brother George on the right. (Courtesy of Linda Poe.)

One of the stores at Gay was built by Olif Litton. This picture was taken in 1963 when the owners were Raymond and Ruth Skinner. The post office was also in the store, and, at one time, a barbershop stood beside the building. The children are Gary and Karen Walters, with a 1954 Chevrolet owned by Tick and Virginia Parsons in the lot.

The Independent Order of Odd Fellows had a lodge at Gay, which was lodge No. 205. An anniversary of the Odd Fellows was held at Gay on April 25, 1919. The district deputy grand master for the fourth district, Herbert Skeen, was the guest speaker. This photograph shows the men of the Gay lodge and Herbert Skeen at their 1919 meeting. (Courtesy of Clement Matheny.)

Logging is a dangerous job today, but in the early 1900s, the work was all done with oxen. The Mitchell brothers are using their team of oxen to haul logs at Gay. They are working on the C. W. Tolley farm on Billy's Run. (Courtesy of Don Flesher collection.)

Nester Godbey is driving Russell Board around Gay in 1920. In February 1937, Godbey and his brothers were working in Parkersburg during the flood that hit the Ohio Valley. His father passed away at Gay, and a radio station was asked to broadcast the news. The brothers heard the news and, after a boat ride and walking through the hills, arrived in time for the funeral. (Courtesy of David Board.)

Working families in rural areas never had extra money for luxuries. In bygone days, it was common for children to share toys, especially bicycles. From left to right, Willie Rhodes, Otta McCrady, and Oris McCrady of Gay prepare to share rides in 1913. (Courtesy of Linda Poe.)

These young ladies enjoy the day at Statts Mill *c.* 1915. On the left is Opal McCrady Rhodes, whose father was James McCrady, a storekeeper in Gay and Statts Mill. On the right is Delpha Rhodes Morris, whose family owned an interest in the F. A. Casto and Company Store. (Courtesy of Linda Poe.)

The early roads in Jackson County were impassable throughout most of the year. The men were required to work on the roads in their precinct with the county road supervisor overseeing the progress. This early photograph of Brush Run shows how narrow the roads were and how hard it was to travel. (Courtesy of Linda Poe.)

The oldest store in Gay was owned by Hershel and Nida Tolley in the 1940s. They lived in the home beside the store, and Arthur Hinzman had a barbershop in a small building beside the house. Here Dorothy Reed Reynolds (left) and Norma Jean Tolley Reynolds have fun in front of the gasoline pumps. (Courtesy of Marie Reed.)

Another covered bridge in Jackson County was at Odaville spanning Sand Creek. The state road commission allowed most of the covered bridges to fall into disrepair, so on September 1, 1959, the old Odaville Bridge fell into Sand Creek. This photograph shows the bridge in need of repair, with an unidentified man on the left and James Riggs on the right. (Courtesy of Bill Mullins.)

Early Ravenswood had several family-owned businesses, including the DeNoon Brothers Drug Store on Sand Street. Here the brothers enjoy a ride through Ravenswood in their two-horse buggy. The streets were unpaved at this time, which made mud a problem for travelers. (Courtesy of Don Flesher collection.)

Jackson County's men fought in the Civil War on both sides. In the early 1900s, a group from Parkersburg organized a reunion for each side. The first Blue and Gray Reunion in Ravenswood was held in August 1913. Each year, the reunion was held in either Spencer or Parkersburg, with the Jackson County men attending. By 1919, the Ravenswood reunion totaled more than 5,000 people. (Courtesy of the Statts Mill Store.)

The area of Belgrove came into existence when a post office opened in 1885 with Daniel Williams as postmaster. Like most areas of Jackson County, Belgrove was self-sufficient. This 1912 photograph shows members of the Fields, Crihfield, Haynes, Rhodes, Jones, Casto, and Westfall families. (Courtesy of Mrs. Delmer Fields.)

On March 23, 1958, Wesley Poe and Linda McCrady were married in the Ripley Tabernacle Parsonage by Rev. H. C. Stanley. The honeymooners spent their first day at the McCrady home in Gay. (Courtesy of Linda Poe.)

This photograph is of the Women's Club of Ripley in 1939. From left to right are the following women: (seated) Madeline Straley, Phyllis Brownell, Madaline Parsons, Alice Shinn, Dorothy Snaith, Corinne Fisher, Ulah Flinn, Hazel Hyre Creel, Mary Lester, Blondena Vineyard, Genevieve Starcher, Jessie Cleek Gilbert, Viletta Armstrong, Edna Casto, and Winnie Kerwood; (standing) Bess Pfost, Katie Kessel, Thelma Casto, Winifred O'Brien, Gladys McConkey, Frances Burdette, Allie Staats, Mollie Armstrong, Ocie King, Violet Hockenberry, Louise Crow, Koontzie Harrison, and Anne McCauley. (Courtesy of Paul King.)

One of the most historical and recognizable objects in Ripley is what is known as "big rocks." The rocks are at the end of the Ripley City Park on the hill overlooking the town. This 1906 postcard has the rocks named as Walters Rocks.

Jakes Baker was born in Angerona and never married. He lived his entire life on his parents' farm along with his two brothers, Benton and Russ. Here Jake is driving his horse-drawn wagon to town for supplies. (Courtesy of Don Flesher collection.)

The public water pump on Walnut Street in Ravenswood was located in front of the Henry Fitzhugh home, which was built in 1832 and is known as the oldest building in Ravenswood. This picture was taken in 1863 when the Flemings owned the home. (Courtesy of Don Flesher collection.)

This picture was taken at the Grass Lick Baptist Church in 1949. From left to right are the following church members: (first row) Patricia Boggess Jones, Audrey Shafer Thacker, Darrell Shafer, and Henry Winter; (second row) Eula Shafer Thacker, Sandy Stover Bailey, Bill Winter, Jo Ann Landfried Raines, Sharon Austin Lanham, Jeanie Austin Parsons, Mae Boggess, and Ruth Ann Skeen Casto; (third row) Guy E. Landfried and Patty Stover Smith. (Courtesy of David Winter.)

Ripley Rotary Club of 1929 members are, from left to right, as follows: (first row) H. Floyd Pfost, Charles Shinn, J. Luther Wolfe, Theo Sayre, George Crow, and Cornelius Staats; (second row) Marion Pfost, John Keenan, Harry Armstrong, Kenna Hyre, Fred Wolfe, Roush Vance, and George Straley; (third row) George Johnson, Okey Hockenberry, J. L. McKitrick, Grover Castrup, R. L. Custer, Samuel Starcher, and Charles Baker; (fourth row) Oshel Staats, Sylvester Sayre, Earl Wright, Dr. Thomas Rymer, Everette Parsons, and G. Burton Crow. (Courtesy of Don Flesher collection.)

When the Gilmer, Ripley, and Ohio Turnpike was completed in 1853, there was a street leading to Mill Creek, but travelers had to cross by a ford in the creek. The covered bridge connecting Bridge Street and West Ripley was built in 1856 by B. R. Cunningham. This photograph shows a baptism being conducted at the ford in Big Mill Creek. (Courtesy of Fred Rhodes.)

Early history of Jackson County stated that every financially secure man between the ages of 21 and 50 was required to do two days work on roads in his precinct between the first of April and the first of September. In 1913, the West Virginia legislature created the State Road Bureau and provided state prison labor for the road work. The State Road Commission was organized in 1916 with the commissioners being political appointees. This created a political workforce of republicans when there was a republican governor, and democrats when there was a democratic governor. This picture shows the State Road Commission employees in Ripley on June 19, 1950, during the democratic governor Okey Patterson's administration. This political commission came to an end on March 11, 1969, when Gov. Arch Moore fired 2,627 state road maintenance employees during a strike. The Civil Service System was created to cover all State Road Commission employees under the new division of highways department.

For years, farm labor was performed by mule, horse, and oxen. In 1940, Wilmer Redman was walking his oxen along Federal Route 21 on the south side of Divide Hill near Kenna. A lady from Ohio snapped this picture of Redman and, after getting his address, mailed him a copy. (Courtesy of Maxine Landfried.)

In 1880, Dr. John Jennings organized the first brass band in Ripley. Members of the band in this 1900 photograph are, from left to right, Cleo Rhodes, Ferdinand R. Hassler, Bob Sayre, Walter W. Armstrong, Rudolph Wright, Charles Starcher, George Kidd, Edward Starcher, Ed Crowley, James Starcher, John Progler, and John Hastings. (Courtesy of Don Flesher collection.)

Ripley Cub Scout Troop No. 103 poses for this 1953 photograph at the Epworth Church. From left to right are as follows: (first row) Eddy Parsons, J. B. Kidd, Charles Snaith, David Parsons, Kenny Batton, Robert Ludwig, Tommy Bates, Bobby Fisher, and Charles Jones; (second row) Charles Heilmann, Dr. Phillip Casto, Kenny Fisher, George Crow, Dick Rader, Robert Cadle, Tom Goodwin, James Patrick Shinn, and George David Reynolds; (third row) Perry Shinn, Guy Fisher, Bob Goodwin, Carmelita Cadle, Bernice Crow, and Wilma Jones. (Courtesy of Don Flesher collection.)

This picture of the Ripley band was taken at the Greer home on Main Street *c.* 1910. From left to right are (first row) unidentified, Fred Riley, Jim Greer, Joe Oldham, and Otmer Riley; (second row) Charles Lerow, O. D. Ripley, H. G. Starcher, C. C. Staats, H. S. Armstrong, and Wilmer Greer. (Courtesy of Don Flesher collection.)

The Alpine Theater was built in 1936 by Holt Rhodes. The movie house closed in 1982 and reopened in 2005. This early 1950s photograph has a group ready for a movie. From left to right are Nancy Thomas, Ann Kessel, Fay Archer, Jim Braden, Freda Mae Matheny, Eddie Braden, Charlotte Skeen, Mary Jo Rhodes, Ethelmae Pickens, and George David Reynolds. (Courtesy of Don Flesher collection.)

In 1920, the Jackson County Courthouse in Ripley was overrun by teachers from across the county. The teachers were in Ripley for the annual teachers' institute. Here the teachers and their spouses pose for the group photograph. As was customary in public, the men wore suits, and women wore their very best dresses. (Courtesy of David Hyre.)

During the height of the Vietnam War, Jackson County did its share to help. This photograph shows military and civic leaders working out plans to ship 2,500 pounds of gifts to the soldiers. At the head table are, from left to right, two unidentified, Deputy Chester McClain, 1st Sgt. Leon Casto, 1st Sgt. Tolbert Walls Jr., and Don Flesher. (Courtesy of Don Flesher collection.)

Ripley had one dance studio for young girls in the early 1950s. The classes were held on the second floor above the Kittle Jewelry Store on Main Street. From left to right, Emily Jenkins, Judy Goodwin, Dixie Walker, Karen Landfried, and Emily Starcher participate in the class of 1952. (Courtesy of Don Flesher collection.)

This photograph in 1953 at Ripley shows the young ladies of Girl Scout Troop No. 1, who are listed here from left to right: (first row) Sarah Sue Rader, Judy Goodwin, Ella Dee Kessel, Emily Lou Jenkins, Peggy Fay Canterbury, Helen Louise Staats, Dixie Lee Walker, and Nancy Sue Parsons; (second row) assistant leader Ireta Goodwin and troop leader Lenore Jenkins. (Courtesy of Emily Lamb.)

In 1909, Ripley had a new steel bridge built by the Canton Bridge Company across Mill Creek. This bridge took the place of the old covered bridge. This picture, taken in 1912, features Audel Harpold Walsh. In March 1948, the entire bridge was torn down, and a new structure was built. (Courtesy of Anne King.)

Virgil S. Armstrong was born in Ripley in 1836 and, by 1861, he was working at the law office of Judge Joseph Smith. Armstrong was a captain in the 17th Virginia Calvary. While in Virginia, he was shot twice. Armstrong became a prosecuting attorney and was elected circuit judge from 1888 through 1896. After his term, he returned to practicing law and did so until 1904. (Courtesy of the Jackson County Public Library.)

On July 25, 1933, deputies George Dudley and Roy Shamblen were transporting prisoner Ralph Harper from Charleston to the state prison in Moundsville. The car was ambushed near Kenna by Charles Harper, Leo Fraser, and Henry Cano. Deputy Shamblen and Ralph Harper were killed. The three were caught and stood trial. Harper and Cano received life sentences, and Leo Fraser received the death penalty.

Members of the Ripley Fire Department are parked on Court Street in 1950. From left to right are the following: (first row) Moss Carney, Paul Lanham, Zeke Tolley, John Karr, John Landfried, Fred Stone, and Gene Straley; (second row) Oris McCrady, Melvin Horn, Skip McGinley, Gene Casto, Jim Heilmann, Bob Richardson, and Clyde Canterbury.

On April 6, 1922, the Rainbow Girls were organized in McAlester, Oklahoma. Girls between the ages of 11 and 20 were sponsored by Masonic organizations. Rainbow teaches girls three basic virtues: faith, hope, and charity. This early 1950s Rainbow Girl group in Ripley shows the elegance of each young lady. From left to right are as follows: (seated) Jean Shinn, Barbara Smith, Jeanne Austin, Imogene Williams, Margaret Staats, Nancy Thomas, Marilyn Miller, and Patty Cox; (second row) Anita Skeen, Jo Ann Hardman, Peggy King, Carol Currey, Ann Kessel, and Shelia Oldham; (third row) Janet Chase, Joyce Kyer, Sandra Landfried, Ella Louise Carney, Bertha Sayre, Judy Kerwood, Ramona Elswick, Sue Click, Naomi Winter, and Bonnie Williams; (fourth row) Peggy Lanham, Dorothy Winter, Jeanne Sallaz, Jo Ann Landfried, Rhonda Harmon, Loretta Jones, Helen Hall, Annetta Stone, Lynne Starcher, and Jackie Whitman. (Courtesy of Don Flesher collection.)

Six

RELIGION AND CHURCH

Religion was the settlers' only true and stable aspect of the early life on the western Virginia frontier. In many counties, the areas were so sparsely inhabited that there were no settled clergy, only the occasional circuit rider. These Methodist preachers usually traveled on a three-week schedule, preaching each day in the area. Some had log camps made that would stand up against the elements and were the central point of all the religious services. The roads were too rough and tents could not be transported; most early preachers rode on horseback. These early log encampments were the predecessors of the tent revivals. Most of the Christians gathered in homes and read the Bible and sang hymns to show their faith. Families used the Bible as a learning tool in early reading; the Bible was the only book families needed and owned. Early churches also doubled as schools, or the school was an addition on the church building.

In Ripley, the first service was preached by Reverend Webster of the Methodist Episcopal Church in 1828. The church was built in 1840, with the Methodist Episcopal Church South getting the property. Ravenswood had its first sermon in 1834 by Reverend Brown, a Presbyterian minister, at the home of Bartholomew Fleming. The first Episcopal church was erected in 1837 and was paid for entirely by Henry Fitzhugh. At Muses Bottom, the first sermon was made in 1812 by a Methodist minister named Turner. The earliest sermon was at Cottageville by a Methodist minister named Noah at the Joseph Parsons home in 1803. These early devotees lead the masses to the religious freedoms welcomed today.

Services at the Grace Episcopal Church in Ravenswood were held at the home of Henry Fitzhugh in 1836. The church was built in 1851, with admission to the diocese in 1852. This picture is of the original building on Washington Street, between Walnut and Sand Streets, *c.* 1890. (Courtesy of Don Flesher collection.)

In 1901, the people of Sandyville built the Methodist Episcopal Church South across from the railroad depot. The church was moved across the road next to the grade school in the 1930s due to an upgrade of Federal Route 21. Today a new and modern church sits only a few yards from where the original church once stood.

In 1866, the Ripley Baptist Church was organized with Jonathan Smith as the pastor. The building pictured was constructed in 1908, with the September 13, 1908, records showing a collection of 71¢. In June 1963, the old church was sold for $12,000 to the Assembly of God Church. Today the building sits empty, awaiting demolition.

The first Methodist Episcopal Church building was erected in 1858, with the present structure constructed in 1899. The dedication services were held on November 4, 1900, by Bishop H. C. Morrison. Fire struck the church on February 9, 1955. Services were held at Ripley High School until the new sanctuary was opened on March 20, 1957. (Courtesy of David Board.)

United Brethren Church and Parsonage, Corner North and Court Streets, Ripley, W. Va. Dedicated October 10, 1926

The United Brethren Church building was constructed in the spring of 1925 by W. L. Pinnell, and the basement was finished in late 1925. The sanctuary and parsonage were completed by the fall of 1926. The project was supervised by Lowell Parsons, Dr. T. L. Miles, and C. C. Staats. The church was formally opened in October 1926 at a total cost of $31,360.

Sunday School Ripley Tabernacle Sept. 23, 1951

In June 1948, Orville Thomas began construction on the Ripley Tabernacle Church with an estimated cost of $20,000. On February 6, 1949, Rev. Delmar Guthrie rang the bell and opened the doors. This photograph shows Reverend Guthrie standing over his flock on September 23, 1951. The original church was demolished in 1987, and a larger building opened in 1989.

Seven

FLOOD AND DISASTERS

The Ohio River has always been the main source of destruction for the Native Americans and later the white settlers. The earliest record of a flood from the Ohio River was in February 1832 with a crest of 49.5 feet. The worst flood in the 1800s was on February 9, 1884, with a crest of 53.9 feet. Then, in March 1907, a flood had a crest of 51 feet. But the worst flood recorded was on March 29, 1913, with a crest of 58.9 feet. These weather bureau records show the flood crests at Parkersburg for each of the floods.

Along with natural disasters, there have been numerous man-made disasters, including the explosion of the James Zearley sawmill on Poplar Fork on April 12, 1892. Almost all the early sawmills were powered by steam, with the boilers the source of the explosions. The operator, Casper Snider, added cool water to the hot boiler. When the water came into contact with the hot boiler, the expanding steam caused the boiler to explode. James Zearley and Casper Snider were both killed as a result of the force of the explosion.

The Ohio River bottom is littered with the skeletons of ships that sank as a result of boiler explosions. By far the most dangerous section of the Ohio River was at Letart Falls. The drop over the falls could only be navigated by an experienced captain, with all others breaking up at the bottom of the falls. As man progressed, the need for better transportation and industry also progressed. This led to the man-made disasters, in addition to natural disasters.

This was all that remained of the Grace Episcopal Church in Ravenswood after a fire on the night of October 7, 1900. Everything was lost including a new organ, with an insurance payout of only $1,000. During the fire, buildings nearby with wooden porches burned. All the graves in the old cemetery behind the church were later moved to the cemetery north of Ravenswood. (Courtesy of the Washington Lands Museum.)

In 1907, near Letart, a freight train traveling to Parkersburg derailed when the fill dirt under the tracks gave way. Engineer Harry Taylor, a fireman, and a brakeman were killed, and the conductor was injured. Taylor's wife sued the Baltimore and Ohio Railroad in 1910 for the sum of $10,000 and won. (Courtesy of John King.)

On September 17, 1915, an engine used on the Ripley and Mill Creek Valley Railway derailed near Ripley Landing at 10:35 a.m. By 8:30 p.m., a wrecking crew was sent from Parkersburg by the Ohio division of the Baltimore and Ohio Railroad to place the engine back on track. While the train was crossing bridge No. 1836 at Ripley Landing, the bridge collapsed, destroying the bridge and injuring nine people. The phone wires for the division office were torn down, which made communications with Parkersburg impossible. It was not until 5:30 a.m. the next morning that a relief train was sent from Parkersburg to rescue the injured and take them to St. Joseph's Hospital in Parkersburg. The wreck resulted in a long delay on all the railroad traffic, because the entire bridge had to be replaced. The span of the bridge had been inspected prior to the collapse and passed inspection. The rapid rate of speed of the train was the contributing factor in the bridge collapse.

STR VIRGINIA STRANDED
IN CORN FIELD AT WILLOW GROVE W.VA.

On Sunday, March 6, 1910, the Pittsburgh and Cincinnati Packet Line met the high water of the Ohio River. The packet *Virginia* became stranded at Willow Grove in a cornfield 600 feet away from the river. The steamboat carried 500 tons of freight and 50 passengers. The steamer rested in the field until the Eichleay Junior Company, a house-moving company from Pittsburgh, arrived on April 21 to refloat the 235-foot-long ship. It was determined that the ship was grounded on an Indian mound. On June 20, after three months of blocking and moving the ship, the Eichleays had the steamer in the river. It cost the Pittsburgh and Cincinnati Packet Line $2,900 for the movers and $500 for the use of the cornfield. The *Virginia* remained in service until it was dismantled in 1929.

The 1913 flood of the Ohio River crested at 58.9 feet, washing away 15 homes and the Baptist church in Millwood. Ripley and Cottageville residents offered to help the marooned families but most took shelter at the schools in Cottageville. This picture shows the Ohio River Railroad employees at Millwood waiting for the rescue boat. (Courtesy of the Jackson County Library.)

The 1913 Ohio River flood devastated the town of Millwood with such severity that every building was damaged. The backwater from the Ohio was so great that Ripley, at a distance of 13 miles, had four feet of water on the dam. Here the Millwood Post Office is completely submerged. (Courtesy of the Jackson County Library.)

On March 19, 1913, one of the worst floods occurred along the Ohio River. At Millwood, the Methodist church, which was constructed in 1899, was severely damaged. The Methodist church was also damaged in the 1937 flood of the Ohio River. As shown here, the church endured the forces of nature and remained open until 1966. (Courtesy of the Jackson County Library.)

The January flood of 1937 took hundreds of lives all along the Ohio River, but no residents of Jackson County were reported drowned. The American Legion Post in Ripley was the first local group to offer help. Food supplies were driven west where boats made their way through Evans to the Millwood area. This photograph shows the Victoria Hotel in Ravenswood. (Courtesy of Betty Fowler.)

116

The 1937 flood of the Ohio River was one of the worst on record at Ravenswood. All the small towns along the river suffered as a result of the sea of water. This photograph shows the powerhouse and the lockmaster's home at the old lock and dam No. 22 at Ravenswood. (Courtesy of Betty Fowler.)

News from Ravenswood during the flood of 1937 told of 20 families being homeless, and the only news reports received were on car radios. It took almost a week before the first Red Cross workers reached Ravenswood. This photograph is looking northwest and shows the Victoria Hotel on the left and the St. Dennis mill in the center. (Courtesy of Betty Fowler.)

The 1937 flood covered a wide area along the Ohio Valley. The main transportation route at the time was the Ohio River Railroad, which ran from Wheeling to Huntington. With the tracks covered at many points along the route, help and supplies were slow to arrive. Here the stranded cars and freight depot at Ravenswood wait for the water to recede. (Courtesy of the Jackson County Library.)

The Ravenswood House was the showplace for the Ohio River traveler, located at Water and Mulberry Streets in Ravenswood. But the Ohio River often damaged the hotel, as shown here during the 1937 flood. During the crest of the flood, water reached the second story. The guests and employees were rescued by Cecil "Cap" Wright, who operated the ferryboat. (Courtesy of Betty Fowler.)

The passenger depot of the Ohio River Railroad in Ravenswood sits submerged in water from the aftermath of the 1937 flood. Due to problems with transportation, the Red Cross did not arrive in Ravenswood until six days after the town was flooded. They had to travel by trails through the hills and around the heads of streams. (Courtesy of Betty Fowler.)

The 1937 flood of the Ohio River brought heartache to all residents along the river. Ravenswood was hit especially hard, with the water cresting over 62 feet. All the homes near the river were underwater. This photograph from Race Street shows the Frank Fleming home, the roof of Emma Rader's home, and the Moore family home on the right. (Courtesy of Betty Fowler.)

During the 1937 flood, the men of Company 1547 at CCC Camp Jackson worked at cleaning and restoring basic needs. Most of the work involved cleaning cisterns so the spread of disease was minimal. Buildings were demolished, drift trash was removed, and homes were cleaned. This photograph shows the Ravenswood Wholesale Grocery on the left and the Frank Fleming house on the right. (Courtesy of Betty Fowler.)

One of the problems in Ravenswood was that the town's water and light plant was underwater. The residents outside the flood zone cared for those who were homeless. Church basements and empty buildings were used to store family belongings. This photograph, taken at Broadway and Mulberry Streets, shows the Orbins Ice Cream Shop and the Victoria Hotel on the left and McMurray's store and family restaurant on the right. (Courtesy of Betty Fowler.)

On April 8, 1953, Sandyville was rocked by an explosion that demolished Gilmore High School. The explosion happened at 6:45 p.m., only 45 minutes after custodians had left, and only three hours after 215 students had left. The new $75,000 auditorium and the main building were destroyed, making the total loss near $200,000. The force blew out the front door and caused the south wall of the main building to crash through the auditorium. When rescue officials arrived on scene, several men found shoes, not realizing the shoes had came from lockers, not victims. Due to the fact there was not any fire, the theory was a natural gas build-up in the walls. Students and teachers had smelled gas earlier in the day, but no major leaks were found. The gymnasium was converted into classrooms, and within a week class had resumed. (Courtesy of Don Flesher collection.)

On February 9, 1955, a fire started in a robe room of the Epworth United Methodist Church in Ripley. The fire spread into the attic and the main sanctuary. During the fire, a missionary study group was holding a meeting in another section of the church. One of the men noticed smoke in the building as he was turning out lights. When he opened the door to the main sanctuary, the heavy smoke rolled. At 8:35 p.m. firemen were alerted, and after two hours of work, the fire was extinguished using 50,000 gallons of water. The main building was severely damaged, and the estimated loss totaled $90,000, but the new annex was saved. Reverend Fuqua and church leaders quickly led efforts to rebuild, and within two years, a new sanctuary had emerged from the ashes and services resumed. (Courtesy of Don Flesher collection.)

Eight

FAIRS AND FESTIVALS

The first fairs in Jackson County were geared toward agricultural products and farm exhibitions. The first fair was held in 1877, and the event was free of charge. There were several fairs in the late 1800s, all with names relating to farming. In 1890, the Jackson County Farmers Stock and Mechanical Exposition Association held a fair, along with the Ravenswood District Exposition and Fair Association, which held its event in 1886. The first fair held at the Ripley Fairgrounds was in 1910. In September 1888, during fair time, the first train entered Ripley. This allowed people who would not have seen the train a chance to witness history. Evans also had a rather large fairground, with grandstands and a horse track. The Staats family held their 1928 reunion at Evans, with several thousand people attending. By the early 1920s, the community of Kenna held its annual fair at the Greene farm. The Kenna fair and the Ripley fair eventually merged to form the Jackson County Junior Fair.

During the Ripley Fair on September 13, 1912, an aviator named Earl Sandth was to perform two flights over the fairgrounds. The first flight of his wooden biplane was uneventful with three passes over Ripley. During the second flight later in the day, Sandth made a dive toward the crowd. When the aeroplane made its circle and approached for landing, his speed was excessive. The plane bounced on the rough ground and crashed through a fence, destroying a section of the wing supports. Sandth was uninjured, but the plane was damaged beyond repair.

On July 4, 1919, Ripley held its largest Independence Day celebration in the town's history. It was requested that all veterans and Red Cross nurses wear their uniforms to the parade, including veterans of the Spanish-American War. The program included prizes for the mother and father who had the most boys in World War I. This photograph shows the work being done on the new courthouse. (Courtesy of the Jackson County Library.)

The first Kenna Fair opened on September 18, 1919, at the Greene farm. The crowd numbered in the thousands on each day. The judges from Morgantown awarded prizes for best purebred cattle, calves, and yearling heifers. The Kenna Fair lasted 10 years, and, in 1929, merged with the Ripley Fair. (Courtesy of Guy E. Landfried.)

This 1937 Fourth of July celebration started at 10:30 a.m. with a parade that ran from North and Seventh Streets, proceeded west to Court Street, south to Main Street, east to Church Street, and then back to North and Seventh Streets. Boxing matches were held in the afternoon, and a pickpocket slipped throughout the crowd stealing a total of $516. (Courtesy of Don Flesher collection.)

The Jackson County Fair, which started in 1927, was held annually at the Evans Fairgrounds. The 1941 fair opened on Tuesday, August 26, with the Ripley Band and a contest for fiddlers. Crowds gathered on Wednesday to see the hot air balloon ascension in the evening sky. On Friday, crowds gathered to see the West Virginia Auto Racing Association's two-heat car race. (Courtesy of Don Flesher collection.)

125

On September 7, 1941, while the Japanese were attacking Pearl Harbor, a U.S. airplane dropped a bomb on a two-man submarine near the island of Oahu. The submarine later washed up on a reef. One Japanese officer was taken prisoner, and the mechanic was never found. The submarine carried two 18-foot-long torpedoes and a 300-pound nitroglycerin charge for self-destruction. The Treasury Department took possession of the craft, and it was used to promote the war department. The 81-foot submarine toured the United States as an advertisement to sell war bonds. On June 23, 1943, almost 5,000 people waited in Ripley to see the craft and to look inside by buying a war stamp. The tractor-trailer parked in front of the courthouse at exactly 10:00 a.m. and left at exactly 10:30 a.m. that next day. Ripley employees were given an hour of holiday time, and schools brought their students to view the submarine. (Courtesy of the Don Flesher collection.)

Ravenswood held its centennial celebration over a six-day period in July 1952. All males residing in Ravenswood had to grow a beard, unless they already had facial hair. Men who wanted to shave after May 26 had to obtain a razor permit costing $2. Events included a fireworks show, marble tournament, rodeo, concerts, and a parade. (Courtesy of the Jackson County Library.)

Ripley High School always promoted a homecoming football game and a homecoming game parade. This 1954 parade proceeded along Main Street moving east in front of the post office. Some of the businesses at the time were the Thomas Meat Market, Charles Kittle Jewelry, McCoy's Clothing, and the Smoke Shop. (Courtesy of the Don Flesher collection.)

Visit us at
arcadiapublishing.com